Translated from the Spanish *Ballenas, vida secreta* by Paula Meiss

First published in the United Kingdom in 2021 by
Thames & Hudson Ltd, 181A High Holborn, London WC1V 7QX

First published in the United States of America in 2021 by
Thames & Hudson Inc., 500 Fifth Avenue, New York, New York 10110

British Library Cataloguing-in-Publication Data.
A catalogue record for this book is available from
the British Library

Library of Congress Control Number 2020949591

ISBN 978-0-500-65267-1

Printed in Spain

Be the first to know about our new releases,
exclusive content and author events by visiting
thamesandhudson.com
thamesandhudsonusa.com
thamesandhudson.com.au

The Secret Life of Whales

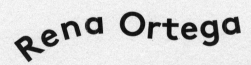

Rena Ortega

THE CETACEAN FAMILY

From the Latin cetus: *"whale" / from the Greek* ketos: *"big fish"*

Whales are some of the largest creatures that have ever lived on earth. The blue whale, for example, can reach up to 110 ft in length and weighs as much as 36 elephants.

Millions of years ago, the ancestors of whales had legs and walked on land. Although whales have adapted to live under water, they still retain some of the features of land mammals.

Whales, dolphins and porpoises belong to a family of animals called cetaceans. Like all mammals, they need to breathe air and when they give birth to their young, the calves feed on their mother's milk. All cetaceans are great at communicating with each other and some of them hunt using echolocation.

CETACEA

Cetacea is the order of mammals that includes whales, dolphins, and porpoises. It is divided into three groups.

ARCHAEOCETI †	MYSTICETI	ODONTOCETI
Ancient whales (now extinct)	Baleen whales	Toothed whales
	Balaenidae	Delphinidae
	Balaenopteridae	Iniidae
	Eschrichtiidae	Monodontidae
	Neobalaenidae	Ziphiidae / Kogiidae
		Phocoenidae
		Physeteridae

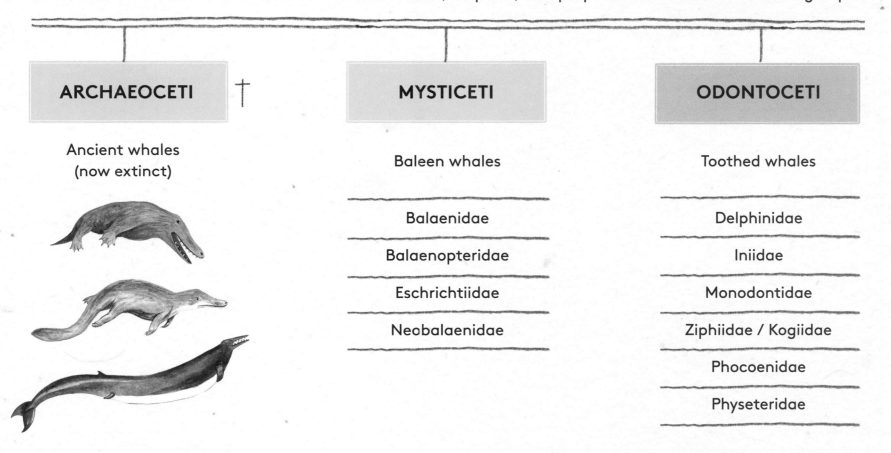

BALEEN WHALES

Kingdom: Animalia
Phylum: Chordata
Subphylum: Vertebrata
Class: Mammalia
Order: Artiodactyla
Suborder: Whippomorpha
Infraorder: Cetacea
Parvorder: Mysticeti

The group of whales known as baleen whales does not have teeth. Their name comes from the fact that their mouths are filled with comb-like plates called baleen. Although they can be found in many places around the world, most species find their food in cold temperate and polar waters. Their upper limbs have evolved into flippers. When they are swimming, their flippers move constantly; they move their tails or flukes vertically to push themselves forward, and use their pectoral fins for steering. Baleen whales have two blowholes to breathe through. Here are some of the whales included in this group.

BALAENIDAE

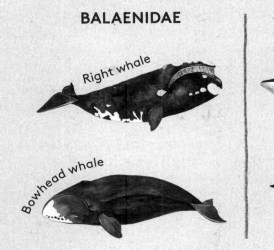

Right whale

Bowhead whale

BALAENOPTERIDAE

Fin whale

Humpback whale

ESCHRICHTIIDAE

Gray whale

NEOBALAENIDAE

Pygmy right whale

TOOTHED WHALES

Kingdom: Animalia
Phylum: Chordata
Subphylum: Vertebrata
Class: Mammalia
Order: Artiodactyla
Suborder: Whippomorpha
Infraorder: Cetacea
Parvorder: Odontoceti

Whales in this group have teeth instead of baleen plates. They may have many teeth or just a single pair, as beaked whales do. They have a single blowhole and a bulge of fatty tissue on their forehead called the melon, which is used for echolocation. Toothed whales are all carnivores: they eat meat. Here are some examples of whales in this group.

DELPHINIDAE

Oceanic dolphins and orca (killer whale)

INIIDAE

Pink river dolphin

MONODONTIDAE

Beluga whale

Narwhal

ZIPHIIDAE

Beaked whale

PHOCOENIDAE

Porpoise

KOGIIDAE

Dwarf and pygmy sperm whale

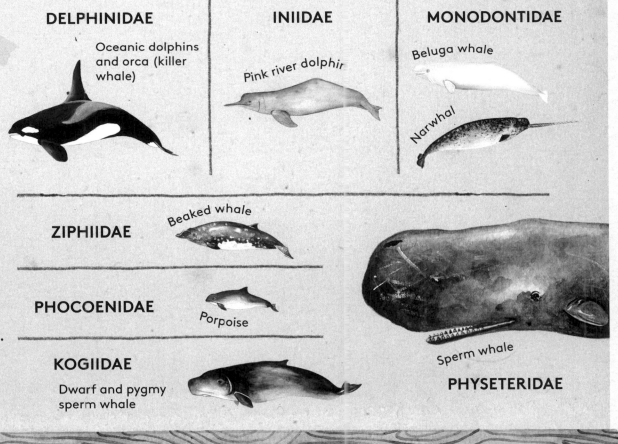

Sperm whale

PHYSETERIDAE

PALEOCENE

EOCENE

Mesonychids

The story of whales begins with the artiodactyls. These are a family of hoofed animals that walk on an even number of toes.

These animals had distinctive thick bones inside their ears, which whales still have today. They were semiaquatic and lived in freshwater habitats.

Indohyus

Pakicetus

The whales' ancestors began to live in places with brackish (saltier) water and their bodies adapted to this habitat.

Ambulocetus

They developed long, strong tails and long limbs.

Kutchicetus

They now lived in saltwater habitats. Their nose openings began to move toward the top of their heads, instead of being at the front, while their eyes moved to the sides of their heads.

Basilosaurus

Their tails adapted to move through water more easily. Their hind legs grew shorter.

OLIGOCENE

WHALE EVOLUTION

The first ancient whales evolved more than 50 million years ago from meat-eating land mammals. Fossils show us that over thousands of years, the feet they once used for running slowly adapted to become better at swimming, growing longer and flatter and eventually turning into fins.

The whale's closest living relative is the hippopotamus. Whales and hippos share ancestors, the artiodactyls. They also have special adaptations for life in the water, including no fur and no sweat glands.

Hippopotamus

Hind legs have completely disappeared.

Mysticeti: whales with baleen plates to filter food

Their bodies began to grow longer. They kept their teeth.

The nose opening is now further up the head.

Odontoceti: whales with teeth to eat smaller sea animals

Dorudon

Echolocation skills for hunting and finding their way underwater have evolved. The blowhole is now right on top of the head.

BALEEN WHALES

Double blowhole with a powerful
spout of up to 33 ft high

Baleen
plates

Small dorsal fin

These ventral
folds help to push
out the water
when the whale
takes in food.

THE BLUE WHALE

This is the largest animal ever to live on Earth. With a weight
of more than 190 tons, it can measure up to 110 ft long. Like all
baleen whales, it feeds on tiny shrimp-like animals called krill,
which it filters by using its baleen plates like a sieve.

Baleen whales have
two blowholes.

These rough patches of skin are often found
on the heads of right whales and gray whales.
They are covered in barnacles and lice. Although
their true function is not known, they can be
used to identify each whale, like fingerprints.

Baleen plates are used to filter krill and
fish out of the water. Between 300 and
400 plates grow down from the upper
jaw. They are made from keratin, like our
nails and hair. The blue whale's baleen
plates can be up to 3½ ft long.

TOOTHED WHALES

Single blowhole, slightly to the left

Huge barrel-shaped head

Triangular or rounded hump

Teeth to eat fish, giant squid and seals

THE SPERM WHALE

This is the world's largest toothed predator. It has the biggest brain in the animal kingdom, weighing up to 18 lb! It can dive to depths of up to 7,400 ft and can be very loud, making sounds of up to 230 decibels underwater. As you can see in the picture, its body is often covered in scars. These come from fighting with giant squid, which it likes to feed on.

The sperm whale only has teeth in its lower jaw. They are very large and heavy, weighing almost 2 lb each!

Toothed whales and dolphins have a single blowhole.

The narwhal lives in Arctic waters, very close to the polar ice cap. Male narwhals grow a long ivory tusk that can be up to 10 ft long!

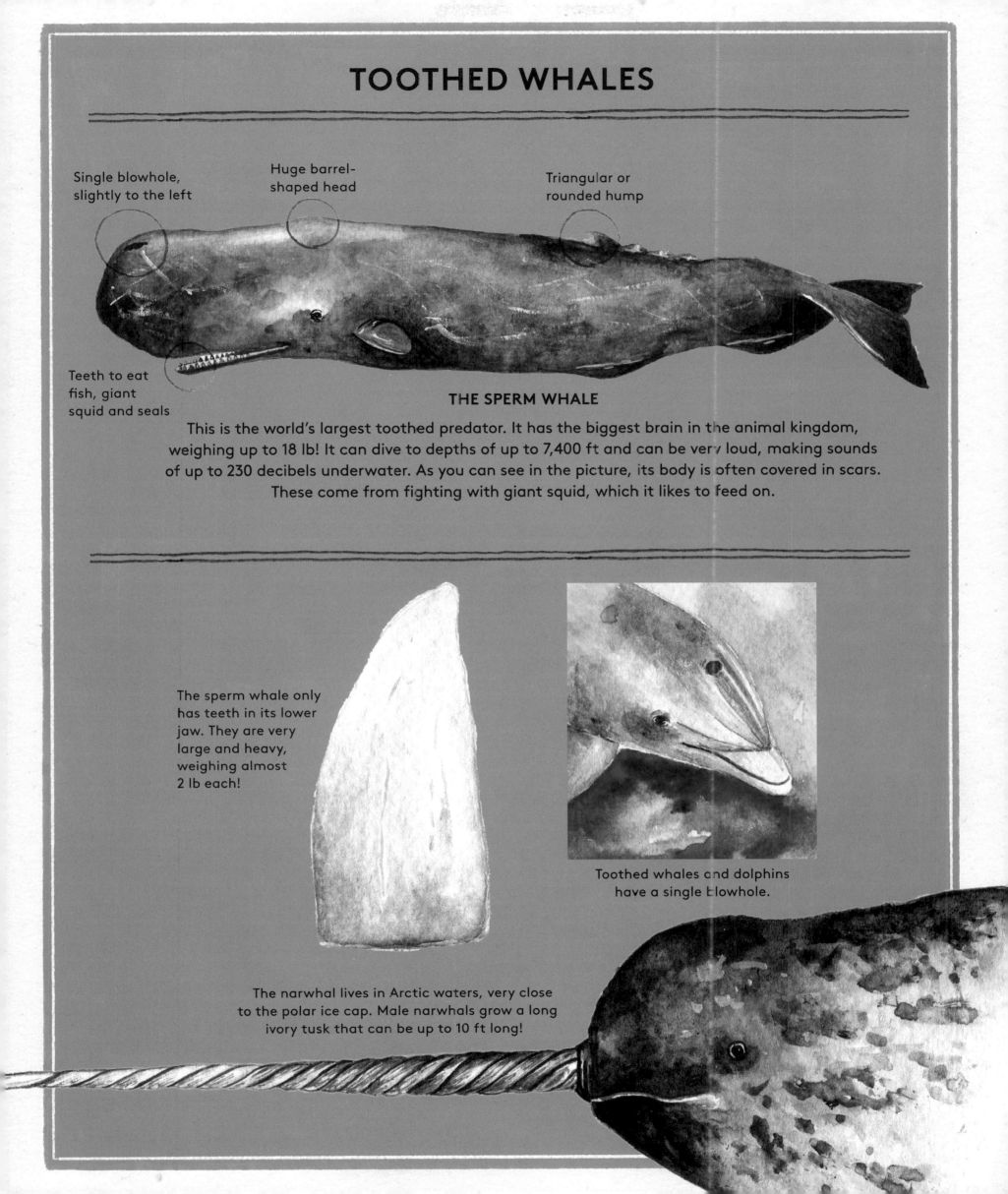

BALEEN WHALES

1. Bowhead whale (60 ft, 100 tons)   **2.** Southern right whale (49 ft, 40 tons)   **3.** Gray whale (40 ft, 20 tons)
4. Fin whale (80 ft, 70 tons)   **5.** Blue whale (110 ft, 170 tons)   **6.** Minke whale (26 ft, 10 tons)
7. Humpback whale (52 ft, 36 tons)   **8.** Sei whale (66 ft, 45 tons)

TOOTHED WHALES

9. Beluga whale (18 ft, 1.6 tons) **10.** Sperm whale (67 ft, 50 tons) **11.** Narwhal (14½ ft, 1.6 tons)
12. Hector's dolphin (5¼ ft, 130 lb) **13.** Blainville's beaked whale (15 ft, 1 ton)
14. Cuvier's beaked whale (21 ft, 3 tons) **15.** Vaquita (5 ft, 110 lb) **16.** Pilot whale (23½ ft, 3.2 tons)
17. Harbor porpoise (5 ft, 120 lb) **18.** Orca or killer whale (26¼ ft, 5.4 tons)

MIGRATION ROUTES

Whales move across the ocean with two basic goals: to look for food in cold waters during the summer, and to mate and breed in warm waters during the winter. With this map, you can follow the routes they take. The yellow dots show the feeding areas, while the pink dots show the breeding grounds. You can see how far they travel along. It's not clear how they learn these migration routes. What we think is that they use the Earth's magnetic field to navigate their environment, like migrating birds. Many species of whales have magnetite crystals in their brains that may help them to sense the Earth's magnetic field.

EASTERN PACIFIC

Humpback whale

DEEP WATERS

SPERM WHALE

- Breeding areas
- Feeding areas
---- Migration routes of more than 5,000 miles

ARCTIC

Beluga whale

Orca

NARWHAL

WESTERN PACIFIC

GRAY WHALE

REEFS

ANTARCTIC

SOUTHERN RIGHT WHALE

WHY DO WHALES MIGRATE?

From June to November, whales usually stay in warm water areas. For example, thousands of humpback whales travel to Tonga, a group of around 170 islands in the South Pacific, of which only 35 are inhabited. That's where they go to mate and give birth.

During the 4-8 months they spend in warm waters for mating, humpback whales don't eat a thing! Nor do they eat while they're migrating. For all that time, they live off the fat reserves that are stored in their bodies.

In the summer, there is plenty of food all around and the waters of southwest Alaska are full of good things to eat, so it's well worth the long journey to go there.

It takes about 30 days for a whale to swim from Hawaii to Alaska.

When they first reach the cold waters to feed, they are hungry and relatively weak. During their first few weeks in the feeding areas, they eat day and night, guzzling up to one ton of fish and krill per day.

Once they reach the feeding areas, mother whales begin to wean their calves. At the same time, the calves learn to hunt by imitating their mothers.

Why do humpback whales make such a tough journey every year? Why don't they stay in cold waters where there is plenty of food or in warm waters where it's nice and comfortable? The answer is to save energy. They migrate to the tropics to spend the winter there, because the waters become too cold to stay at the poles.

Whale calves don't have a thick enough layer of fat to spend the winter in cold water or survive under harsh conditions. They need to be somewhere where they can eat huge quantities of food in just a few months. Adult whales grow a layer of fat about 6 in. thick.

PECTORAL FINS

These fins are the whale's front limbs. They work like oars, moving back and forth as the whale glides through the water. Humpback whales are part of a genus called Megaptera, which means "big wings:" this is because their pectoral fins are very long in proportion to their bodies. The edges of their fins are lined with bumps called tubercles, which help the fins to move smoothly through the water.

White-striped pectoral fin of a minke whale

DORSAL FIN

This fin is on the whale's back and helps to keep it stable while it's swimming. The size, position and shape of the dorsal fin are different depending on the species of whale.

Rounded
Hector's dolphin

Triangular
Sperm whale, gray whale

Hook
Blue whale, minke whale, humpback whale

Long
Orca

Blue whale

Right whale

Minke whale

Humpback whale

Southern right whales and bowhead whales don't have dorsal fins. This adaptation is caused by their environment: since they always live in cold waters, it stops them from losing heat.

TAIL FIN

Unlike fish and sharks, whales have tail fins, also called flukes, which are oriented horizontally, not vertically. Combined with the whale's powerful muscles, a whale's tail not only helps it to reach high speeds but also to keep a constant rhythm during its long migrations. The shape of the flukes varies a lot from one species to another. In fact, you can identify a whale's species just by looking at its tail.

Look at these tail fins. What differences can you spot? The narwhal's fluke looks like it's facing the wrong way, but this helps it to swim in reverse if it gets caught in ice. No two humpback whale tails are the same! The markings on the underside of the fluke are unique to each whale, like human fingerprints.

Sperm whale

Gray whale

Orca

Beluga whale

Narwhal

A COMPARISON OF SIZES

Human: 6 ft

Giant Pacific octopus: 32 ft

Ocean sunfish: 11 ft

Blue whale: 110 ft

Whale shark: 61½ ft

Sperm whale: 67 ft

Lion's mane jellyfish: 120 ft

Giant squid: 40 ft

Great white shark: 23 ft

Colossal squid: 13½ ft

Giant oceanic manta ray: 23 ft

WHALE BEHAVIOR

Studying animals that spend most of their time deep in the ocean can be tricky. However, the time that whales spend on the surface is key to understanding their behavior. Here are some of the most striking things to look out for.

LOBTAILING

Lobtailing or tail-slapping is when the whale raises its fluke out of the water and slaps it forcefully on the surface.

FLIPPER-SLAPPING

Humpbacks will often roll onto their side or back and noisily slap the surface of the water repeatedly with one or both fins.

BREACHING

This is the most spectacular thing that whales do! The whale uses its tail to leap through the air, pushing most of its body out of the water. It's also called cresting.

HEAD SLAP

A head slap is when a whale lunges out of the water and strikes the underside of its chin forcefully on the surface.

ROUNDING OUT

This is when whales arch or hump their backs, showing their dorsal fins as they prepare for a deep dive.

BLOW

The blow is one of the easiest ways to spot a whale in the ocean. The term refers both to the act of breathing itself (an explosive outward breath followed by an inward breath) and to the cloud of water droplets created above the whale's head when it breathes out.

No one knows what makes this water cloud so easy to see. It includes water vapor that condenses in the cold air, but it may also contain mucus from the whale's lungs. Sometimes it is called a spout.

LOGGING

Logging is when whales rest by lying close to the surface of the water with their dorsal fin and part of their back in the open air. They kind of look like logs floating in the sea.

TUSKING

Male narwhals fight by rubbing their tusks together, which makes a sound like two wooden sticks hitting each other. Scientists think this is how they decide who's in charge in their social group. Sometimes more than two whales fight at the same time and sometimes a third turns up just to watch.

FLUKING

When a large whale is getting ready to dive, it arches its back, pushing the central part of its body above water to get a better downward angle. When its head is in the right position, the whale dives down. The last thing you see is its tail fluke sticking straight up above the water.

SPYHOPPING

A spyhop is when a whale rises vertically to the surface and pokes its whole head out of the water. They do this to check where they are and see what's going on.

The right whale and the gray whale have a very similar and characteristic V-shaped blow. For right whales, it is usually higher and wider, since their blowholes are further apart. The gray whale's blow is usually heavy and sometimes heart-shaped.

The blow of the humpback whale is similar to that of the sperm whale. It is just as heavy and wide, but taller and more vertical, reaching a height of 10 ft.

The sperm whale has just one blowhole, slightly to one side of its head. Its unusual blow is low and wide and is directed forward and to the left.

THE BLOW

The blow is a good way to tell different species of whales apart. The blue whale produces the most spectacular blow. It is a vertical column of spray that can be more than 30 ft high!

HOW WHALES SLEEP

Whales may be one of the least sleep-dependent animals in the world. Sperm whales only spend 7% of their day asleep, and that time is broken into short naps that last between 10 and 15 minutes. They always stay close to the surface so that they can keep breathing.

One of the most curious facts about sleeping whales is that sperm whales rest in groups called pods, floating upright in the water. However, not all whales do this: the vast majority sleep in a horizontal position.

Whales can take in more air in one breath than many animals, since their lungs are proportionately larger. To breathe, whales come up to the surface, take a breath, and then dive back down to the same position to continue sleeping. While they sleep, half of their brain stays awake, allowing them to watch out for predators, maintain social contact, control their breathing, and keep swimming. It seems pretty complicated, but this is how whales rest!

THE DIVE SEQUENCE

1. When the whale comes to the surface to breathe, its blowhole is the first thing to rise out of the water. It immediately takes several breaths.

Orcas hold their breath underwater. They open their blowhole and begin to breathe out just before reaching the water's surface. The resting breathing rate of an orca is around 3 to 7 breaths every 5 minutes.

The longest that a sperm whale can stay under water is around 2 hours. The gap between dives can be up to one hour, but it usually lasts between 5 and 10 minutes. Sperm whales are one of the species that dive the deepest.

2. As the whale's dorsal fin begins to show, its sloping back forms a triangle with the surface of the sea. As the whale starts to dive, it arches its back and its tail fluke rises slowly into the air.

3. The fluke rises above the surface as the whale dives, and the underside of the tail becomes visible. This is a sign that the whale is about to make a deep dive that may last between 5 and 40 minutes, reaching a maximum depth of 400 ft.

Sperm whales can dive more than 3,000 ft below the surface in search of squid. The whale will often hold its breath for up to 90 minutes during a dive of this kind.

The longest a human being has ever held their breath underwater is 19 minutes.

HOW WHALES FEED

Baleen whales trap large amounts of food at once by filtering water with their baleen plates. They usually eat 4% of their body weight every day.

Toothed whales use echolocation to find their prey. This sense works like a sonar: the sound bounces off the prey and an echo comes back to the whale. It lets whales work out the size, shape, distance and speed of their prey.

Orcas are predators that feed on fish, squid, sea lions and even on other whales. They use their teeth to hunt and kill their prey. They don't chew their food, they just swallow it in one piece!

Krill are small shrimp-like animals about 1½ in. long. They are the favorite food of blue whales, who can take in up to 90 tons of water, filled with krill, by opening their mouth and lunging forward.

3. Once the fish reach the surface, the humpback whales lunge up in formation and feed together.

2. The bubbles confuse the prey. The other whales help by blowing even more bubbles, forcing the trapped fish to try to escape by swimming up to the surface.

1. Humpback whales are famous for a hunting technique called "bubble net" feeding. One of the whales starts blowing a circle of bubbles to create a barrier that keeps small fish trapped inside.

WHALE SONG

Singing is one of the most surprising talents that these huge animals possess. In fact, whale songs are some of the most complex sound compositions found in the animal kingdom. The songs are usually performed to attract a mate. It's the males who sing to attract the females, who can hear them up to 18 miles away.

Whales don't have vocal cords, so they make the sounds using a series of cavities or sacs inside their throat. These allow them to move air around without losing it underwater.

SONOGRAM

A sonogram is a way of showing sounds as an image. This sonogram represents a whale song. Whale songs are divided into themes and phrases that are repeated over and over, and a single song can last between 6 and 35 minutes. A humpback whale can sing for up to 22 hours!

FAMILIES AND SOCIETY

Whales have some of the most complex social lives in the animal kingdom. Orcas, for example, always travel in groups or pods: they share strong social bonds with each other, just like wolves in a pack. This helps them to hunt, migrate, share food and protect each other.

female beluga whale

Male dorsal fin

Female dorsal fin

Orcas

When the males and females of the same species look different, it's called sexual dimorphism. Male orcas have a longer and more pointed dorsal fin than female orcas.

Narwhals

Although female narwhals can sometimes grow them too, tusks are most frequently found on male narwhals. In fact, they sometimes grow two tusks! Narwhals tend to form small groups, which are often of the same sex (all males or all females with their calves). During autumn migrations, many groups swim together for very long distances. Their long tusks can be seen on the surface when they come up to breathe.

Beluga whales

Beluga whales grow paler as they get older. They are a dark shade when they are born but gradually turn lighter, eventually becoming pure white when they are fully grown. Males are larger than females, with bigger heads, and their fins are more curved.

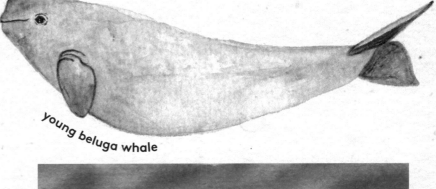

baby beluga whale (calf)

male beluga whale

MOTHERHOOD

Like all mammals, whales give birth to live babies. They usually give birth to just one calf at a time, which comes out tail first, to avoid the risk of suffocation. The calves are fed on their mother's milk, which is thicker and more nutritious than the milk of land mammals.

young beluga whale

Sperm whales

A mother sperm whale often leaves her calf on the surface to be looked after by other female sperm whales. They protect the calf while the mother dives deep below the surface to find food.

Humpback whales

A humpback whale pregnancy lasts for 11 months. When it is born, the calf is nursed for a whole year. For the first two months of its life, it grows up to 1½ in. every day.

WHALE SKELETONS

Side view of skull with baleen plates
BOWHEAD WHALE

Top view of skull
FIN WHALE

Top view of skull
BLUE WHALE

These small bones are usually hidden inside the muscle and fat of the whale's body. They are all that is left of the pelvis (hip bones) that the whale's ancestors with legs once had.

BLUE WHALE skeleton

The skeleton of the blue whale is not as strikingly shaped as those of some other whales, but it's still remarkable for its enormous size and weight. A blue whale skeleton can weigh between 4 and 5 tons. The most notable feature is its huge, wide head, which is bigger than any other whale's.

The sperm whale's spermaceti organ helps it to float in the water. It contains between 3 and 5 tons of waxy liquid called spermaceti.

There are still jointed finger-like bones inside the pectoral fins.

carpals

ulna

humerus

radius

metacarpals

phalanges

The hind legs have completely disappeared. The tail is not made of bone, but of dense tissue that is firm and flexible.

The head of the orca is large and has prominent rows of upper and lower teeth.

The skull of the beaked whale is long and narrow. It has two massive teeth in its lower jaw.

ORCA skull

SPERM WHALE skeleton

This huge skeleton has a spine with 49 vertebrae, ribs that provide flexibility in the pressure of deep water, and a triangular skull with very big jaws.

WHEN SOCIAL TIES TURN DEADLY

When a whale is beached, it sends out signals asking for help. This attracts other whales from the pod, who often try to help their friend. But when the tide goes out, the whales who came to the rescue can easily get stranded themselves. Pilot whales are more likely to become beached in a group because of the strong social bonds between them.

If you see a whale stranded on the beach, what should you do?

• Touch it as little as possible!
• Call the police
• Keep its skin damp

Most whales are crushed to death by their own weight if they can't get back into the water quickly.

WHALES IN DANGER

Although they are well adapted to live underwater, whales are threatened by various natural and human factors. These may block their senses, prevent them from moving or poison their bodies. The dangers are different for each whale species.

Toothed whales find their way using echolocation. They need this sense to survive, but there are some things that can stop it from working properly. One of the most common mistakes that whales can make is getting beached by accident when they're chasing prey or trying to escape from predators, such as orcas. Scientists think that very sandy beaches, made up of fine grains of sand, do not accurately reflect back the signals that the whales send. As a result, the whales get confused and think they are in deep waters. Whales can also make mistakes when swimming near beaches they don't know well, or after a very rough storm.

FISHING NETS

Many sea animals get trapped in abandoned fishing nets. They may be strangled or seriously injured when they try to free themselves. North Atlantic right whales are at particular risk from fishing nets.

A PLASTIC DISASTER

Baleen whales feed by taking in huge amounts of water and filtering out the krill. Unfortunately, this means they can easily end up eating plastic and other waste left in the sea. The growing level of plastic waste in our oceans is a huge problem, because it can fill their stomachs and even block their blowholes.

MICROPLASTICS

Most of the plastics thrown into the sea do not break down completely. Instead, they become small particles known as microplastics. These cause serious pollution in the oceans as they get smaller and smaller but never totally disappear. Every piece of plastic ever made still exists today.

SPERMACETI

Spermaceti is a waxy liquid substance that is found in the head cavities of the sperm whale. Inside a sperm whale's huge forehead is its spermaceti organ, which probably helps to control the whale's buoyancy. As the whale dives deeper, the water gets colder and makes the wax turn more solid.

Before industrial whaling was developed, whales were hunted from small rowing boats. A whaler would take a harpoon and throw it at the whale with all his might, from a distance of 15 to 30 ft. The iron tip, sharp as a blade, would get stuck in the whale's thick layer of blubber.

When this happened, the whole pod of whales would realize they were under attack and would try to get away. As the harpooned whale tried to get rid of the harpoon, it thrashed around, stirring up the waters. The whale would sometimes try to dive deep and sink the hunters' boat. Meanwhile, the crew of around six men struggled to pull the whale out of the water. When it was too tired to fight any more, one of the whalers would stab a long spear into its flesh, again and again, until it finally died.

THE WHALING INDUSTRY

For many hundreds of years, whales were hunted for their meat and their blubber, which could be turned into oil. When the industrial revolution came, whale oil was in such high demand that whaling ships began hunting whales on a massive scale. Eventually the whaling industry wiped out more than half of the world's whales.

In 1712, there were more than a million sperm whales, but by the end of the 20th century, there were only 360,000 left, one third of the original number.

In 1986, the International Whaling Commission (IWC) put a temporary ban on commercial whaling so that whale populations could begin to grow again. However, a few communities, such as the Inuit people of Canada and Greenland, are allowed to keep hunting whales because it is considered an important part of their culture.

Products obtained from the whaling industry:

- **Whale oil:** used for industrial purposes, lighting, and food.
- **Spermaceti:** cosmetics, lipsticks, oil pencils.
- **Ambergris:** the most valuable product from the whaling industry, used to make perfumes.
- **Endocrine glands and liver:** pharmacy products, hormones, vitamin A.
- **Meat:** 1.7% of the meat eaten in Japan comes from whales.

Whales are still hunted today, especially to supply Japan, the country that's the largest consumer of whale meat in the world. Japan left the IWC so that it could begin hunting whales again.

WHALE WATCHING

If you want to go whale watching, it's best to choose a tour that has strict rules about how to approach the whales. It's important to keep your distance and avoid causing stress to these magnificent creatures.

Whale watching is one of the best ways to get to know these amazing animals. You might need to be patient but there are lots of fascinating things to watch out for: blows and spouts, dark shadows moving under the water, flippers, foam and more.

With a little luck, it's possible to see whales in any ocean in the world. But many species tend to visit specific areas at certain times of the year. Here are some of the best places in the world to watch these incredible animals:

- Azores Islands, Portugal

- Bahía Ballena, Costa Rica

- Baja California, Mexico

- Canary Islands, Spain

- Glacier Bay, Alaska

- Hermanus, South Africa

- Hervey Bay, Australia

- Húsavík, Iceland

- Monterey Bay, California

- Puerto Madryn, Argentina

To my parents, for their support and love.
To Mica, for teaching me how to love the sea.
To Húsavík, for showing me the fascinating world of whales.
To Mosquito Books, for making my wish come true.

Rena Ortega

To all of life's changes, because from them, I grow and, like the sea,
they remind me that movement means being wild and alive.

Mia Cassany

Contributors

Micael Vidal Mañá, specialist in pisciculture and aquaculture, Galicia, Spain
Tom Grove, whale biologist, University of Edinburgh, UK: whalewise.org
Cristina Fernández González, biological oceanographer, University of Vigo, Spain
Garðar Þröstur Einarsson, whale specialist, Húsavík Whale Museum, Iceland
Lucie Kessler, masters student in Marine Biology, La Rochelle University, France

The publishers would like to thank Húsavík Whale Museum in Iceland for their invaluable help with this book. Their feedback, advice and fact-checking have helped us to spread awareness, love and respect to a l the whales of the world.